10
Neat Things
About Being a
Flower Girl

Penelope Colville Paine

Itoko Maeno

In loving memory
John H. Paine 1935-2006

Copyright © Penelope Colville Paine
Illustrations Copyright © Itoko Maeno

Published by
Paper Posie, Santa Barbara, CA
(800) 360-1761
See all Paper Posie's products for children at weddings at
www.paperposie.com

Publisher's Cataloging-in-Publication
(Provided by Quality Books, Inc.)

Paine, Penelope Colville, 1946–
    10 neat things about being a flowergirl / by Penelope C. Paine.
    — 1st ed.
    p. cm.
ISBN-10: 0-9707944-1-X   ISBN-13: 978-0-9707944-1-3
    1. Wedding attendants—Juvenile literature. 2. Wedding etiquette—Juvenile
literature. [1. Weddings. 2. Weddings etiquette. 3. Etiquette.] I. Title.
II. Title: Ten neat things about being a flowergirl
BJ2065.W43P35 2002   395'.22
                                                                QBI33-390

Editor: Gail M. Kearns
Layout & Typography: Cirrus Book Design

Printed in China, Shenzhen, Guangdong
04/2010, C&C Offset Printing Co., Ltd.

13 14 15 16 17

This Book Belongs To:

_____

The Bride and Groom Will Be:

_____

Wedding Date:

_____

There are lots of neat things about
being a Flower Girl . . .

1

A Flower Girl is the bride's
special helper

I was a flower girl for my big sister.
Her wedding day was a Saturday.
This is when I usually play soccer but
I had lots of fun at the wedding.

2

A Flower Girl gets to wear
a really cool outfit

I wiggled a lot when I was being
fitted for my flower girl dress.
My aunt had to help me stay still
so that Mom could get the
hem right.

I felt like a cloud
. . . all fluffy and floating.

3

A Flower Girl carries a bouquet
of flowers or a basket of rose petals,
sometimes she wears flowers in her hair

I carried a beautiful basket of pink roses and I had a flower pinned in my hair.

4

Flower Girls get to walk in front of the bride before the wedding ceremony and behind the bride and the groom after they are married.

I knew I would have to walk very slowly in my long dress. At the rehearsal I had to practice going up and down the steps with the bridemaids and groomsmen. They made me giggle a lot!

5

A Flower Girl is in the wedding ceremony

While the bride and groom were saying their vows, I stood as still as I could. Mom and Dad smiled at me and I felt very special. Mom cried when the bride and groom kissed. My mom is like that.

6

A Flower Girl makes new friends

I had to stand with my cousin. He was the ring bearer. I sort of wished that I could carry the rings. We had fun dancing and I stayed up very, very late.

7

A Flower Girl is in the wedding photographs

After the wedding ceremony
we all threw rose petals over the
bride and groom. I was in
LOTS of photographs. Then we
all went in a big limousine to
the reception, where there was
lots of yummy food and a
band played!

8

A Flower Girl gets a gift from the groom

Before the bride and groom went
away on their honeymoon, the groom
gave me a necklace. It was a little
silver basket of flowers on a chain.
I keep it in my jewelry box and,
sometimes I wear it when I go out.

9

A Flower Girl gets to keep her outfit

I kept my pink flower girl dress (and my matching pink shoes) and I put them on when I have my friends over. We pretend to have a store selling gowns, veils and rose petals. One day I'm going to own a real store.

10

A Flower Girl has lots of fun with
her family and friends

I collected autographs from all my relatives. My uncle who lives far away in another country gave me $5.00 because I am saving up to go to science camp in the summer.

SCIENCE CAMP

I liked being a Flower Girl . . .
and I hope you do too!